WISDOM OF THE BUDDHA

(STORIES AND PARABLES)

BY

REYAZ NADEEM

PREFACE

This book is a collection of interesting stories and parables associated with the Buddha. Actually, there is a vast collection of stories and parables attributed to the Buddha, easily available over the net. But many of them just lack common sense and which would make one think whether such things can be really attributed to the wise Buddha. However, here the selections have been made after carefully examining and refining them. As a result, this work becomes intriguing as well as appealing to the masses. There are also some modifications done but without compromising with the essence of the Buddha's message.

REYAZ NADEEM

KOLKATA, INDIA

2018 CE

CONTENTS

CONTENTS

CONTENTS

WISDOM OF THE BUDDHA

(STORIES AND PARABLES)

1

The First Meditation

The Buddha remembered his very first meditation under a rose-apple tree. . . .

It was the day of the first plowing of the fields. The tradition was that people would dress in fine clothes to attend a big ceremony held outside in the fields. Flags and colorful cloths hung from the trees. Many tables were set up as altars upon which the finest foods and drinks were placed. The holy men of the Brahman class would chant prayers to ask for blessings. They prayed that the fields would yield healthy and plentiful crops.

So it was on that day, when Siddhartha was nine, that King Suddhodana, his royal family and all his ministers attended the ceremony. Many children were there. They loved this day because after the prayers and chanting, they were to enjoy the most delicious cakes and sweets. Nevertheless, the prayer readings proved much too long and soon the children tired. The ladies-in-waiting led them to the outer fields to watch the actual plowing. Siddhartha was amongst them.

In the field, a man naked to the waist was prodding a water buffalo to pull a plow. It was very close to noon, and the sun shone relentlessly on his bare back. He was sweating profusely and visibly tired from walking up and down in the field making the furrows. Intermittently, he would whip the reluctant buffalo. The buffalo had to pull very hard with the yoke upon its body. Its hoofs gripped the ground beneath as its large body inched forward dragging the heavy plow behind it. The plow turned up the soil exposing the worms that made their homes there. The worms wriggled in distress trying desperately to find cover. Others worms writhed in pain as they had just been cut in halves. Siddhartha then realized why so many small birds were hovering near the ground. They were eating the live, defenseless worms and other tiny bugs that laid bare for their easy picking. Just then, a hawk swooped down and caught one of the small birds. With its lunch secured in its claws, it took to the air again giving out the loud cry of a master of the sky.

Siddhartha watched in silence. He felt the toil of the man who ploughed the field in the hot sun. He felt the struggle of the water buffalo chained to the plow. He felt the pain of the worms cut by the plow. It was heart wrenching to witness the worms, the insects, and the small bird losing their lives so abruptly. Siddhartha felt their fear, their pain, and the unpredictability of life itself.

The noonday sun was extremely hot. Siddhartha took shelter under a rose-apple tree. The leaves provided a much needed shade away from the heat. He sat down on a stone slab. He curled up his legs to rest on the cool surface of the stone. He straightened his body to gather his breath. He rested his hands on his lap. With his eyes lowered, Siddhartha reflected on the scene that had transpired in the field. He sat detached from the noises of the children laughing and playing around him.

After sitting quietly for a while, Siddhartha noticed that his thoughts subsided. He experienced a calm and clear awareness from within. He recognized that the man, the water buffalo, the birds, and the worms had one thing in common: each of them was tied to the conditions of its life. A worm was tied to the condition that it was a food source for birds. A small bird was bound by the condition that it might fall prey to larger birds. A water buffalo had to live in captivity and work for its captors.

Siddhartha continued to look deeper. He recognized that life conditions brought fear and pain at times, and enjoyment at others. In one moment, the small bird was enjoying the worms, but in the next moment, it was food for the hawk.

Moreover, Siddhartha observed that the conditions were different for everyone. Some animals enjoyed a greater degree of freedom and safety than others. The peacocks of the royal gardens certainly led a better existence than that of a water buffalo. It was the same with people. Some were good looking and some were not. Some were strong while some were weak. Some were smart and some were dumb. One thing stood out above all else: regardless of what conditions they were born with, all living things wanted to live in peace and happiness. All living things wanted to avoid suffering. All living things were thus interconnected with one another through this universal wish to be happy.

Siddhartha himself was no exception. It was through his own experience of heat, pain, fear, and fatigue that he was able to connect with the man, the water buffalo, the worms, and the birds in the field. His want of happiness and his aversion to suffering connected him to the experiences of others. Without the common ground of experience, there could be no connection. Siddhartha remembered the time when he had tried to describe the taste of a sweet dish to his attendant who had never tasted one. He could not.

A very strong conviction then seized Siddhartha. If he wanted to help others, he would need first to find out for himself how he could help. He needed to understand the nature of the conditions that created suffering. Only then would he be able to change them so that every living being could enjoy happiness.

"Siddhartha!" someone shook the Prince's shoulder. King Suddhodana and Queen Gotami both saw Siddhartha sitting under the tree. The Queen was in awe of the fact that a nine year old could sit in a meditation posture so serenely. However, the King's facial expression tensed up right away. In his heart, his greatest fear was taking shape - that Siddhartha would leave him one day in search of the Truth.

...

2

The Savior Prince

One day, Siddhartha was resting under a tree in his father's royal garden and enjoying the peace and beauty of nature. And all of a sudden a swan fell from the sky just in front of him. The bird had been shot at by an arrow which had pierced its body; and the poor creature was fluttering about in great agony.

The kind-hearted prince rushed to the help of the bird. He removed the arrow, dressed its wound, and gave it water to drink.

And carrying the bird in his arms he came back to the place where he had been seated. He wrapped the bird in his upper garment and held it next to his chest to give it warmth and comfort.

The prince was wondering who could have shot this bird, and before long there came his cousin Devadatta armed with bow and arrow. He asked Siddhartha whether he had seen a wounded swan fall from the sky. The young prince replied in the affirmative and showed him the bird which by that time had completely recovered.

Devadatta demanded that the bird be handed over to him

but Siddhartha refused to comply. A sharp argument ensued between the two. Devadatta argued that the bird should belong to him because by the rules of the game, he who kills a game becomes the owner of the game. But the prince denied the validity of the rules, and counterclaimed that it is only he who protects has the right to claim ownership. And neither party would yield.

So both of them decided to go to the king's court where the counsellors argued the merits of each case. In the end the king referred the case to his wisest minister who after examining the pros and cons declared that the bird should belong to him who saved its life rather than one who tried to take it away.

But Devadatta was still adamant in his claim. So the wise judge made Siddhartha and Devadatta stand at a distance apart from each other, and he then put the bird in the middle. And to everyone's surprise, the swan started walking towards its saviour.

Thus the noble prince became the rightful owner of the bird.

•••

3

Mother's Affection

Hariti was a demoness of Rajagriha. She had hundreds of children of her own, whom she loved and doted upon, but to feed them she abducted and killed the children of humans.

The bereaved mothers of her victims shared their loss with the Buddha, and urged him to do something about it so that the other children would be saved from suffering such a cruel fate.

The Buddha, compassionate he was, felt pity on the suffering women, and thought of a plan in order to teach the demoness a lesson. He stole the youngest of Hariti's son by using his supernormal powers, and hid the demon-child under his alms-bowl.

Meanwhile, Hariti desperately searched for her missing son throughout the universe but was not able to find him anywhere. And ultimately, she appealed to the Buddha for help, for the Blessed One at that time was more powerful than any of the humans or jinn.

The Buddha pointed out that she was suffering because she lost one of her hundreds of children, and asked if she could imagine the suffering of parents whose only child had been devoured. Hariti replied contritely that their suffering must be many times greater than hers.

And seeing her remorseful the Buddha returned her child. Hariti's joy knew no bound on being united with her son, for nothing in the world could be compared to the affection of a mother.

And from that time she vowed to protect all children, and in lieu of children's flesh, she promised to eat only pomegranates.

And she was so impressed with the Buddha that she accepted his Dharma and became one of his disciples from the jinn.

•••

4

The Man-Eater

Alavaka was a demon who lived near the city of Alavi and feasted on human flesh. He was very fierce, powerful and crafty.

One day, the king of Alavi went hunting for deer in the jungle and Alavaka caught him. The king begged to be released, but in return for his freedom the demon made a deal that the king had to send one person every day into the jungle as an offering to him. The king fearing for his own life readily agreed to the demon's proposal.

Every day after that, a prisoner would be sent from the palace dungeons into the forest with a plate of rice. The wretched soul was told that to gain freedom he had to go to a certain tree, leave the plate there and then he could go as he pleased.

At first, many prisoners volunteered to go on that "simple" mission. But as the days passed by and no one returned to tell the other prisoners what had happened, the remaining prisoners grew suspicious and had to be forced each day to go into the forest.

Soon the prison became empty. And the king became worried that if Alavaka did not receive his daily quota, he might come and kill him instead. So the fearful king consulted with his ministers who advised him to drop packets of gold in the streets, and those found picking up the packets would be caught as thieves and sent to Alavaka.

But when the word got around nobody dared to collect the packets. As a last resort the king started catching children for offering. And as a result, the terrified inhabitants of the city began to flee, leaving the streets deserted and the king completely desperate. There was only one more boy left, - and he was the king's son. With much reluctance the king ordered that the prince be sent to Alavaka the next morning.

But luckily for the king, that day the Buddha happened to be near the city. When the king heard of his arrival, he went to the Buddha, related his story and pleaded for help.

Out of compassion for the poor souls, the Blessed One turned his steps towards the forest and by evening he managed to reach the entrance of Alavaka's cave.

At that time the demon was away in the mountains, and the Buddha requested the gatekeeper to let him spend the night in the cave. Believing him to be a harmless ordinary human, the demon gatekeeper left his position to inform his master about the visitor's request.

When the gatekeeper was gone, the Buddha out of curiosity entered the cave-house and encountered Alavaka's wives. The demonesses were also surprised to see a human being inside their dwelling.

And the Blessed One took the opportunity, sat on Alavaka's seat, and started preaching the Dharma to the well-behaved jinn-ladies.

Meanwhile, Alavaka on learning about a human visitor hurried back home. And finding the human seated on his seat and talking to his wives, Alavaka became so angry that he created a loud terrifying sound which shook and rattled the whole forest.

But the Blessed One was unafraid and unmoved.

Alavaka then attacked the Buddha by throwing his spear and club at him. But to his surprise, the weapons instead of harming the Blessed One fell close to his feet.

Witnessing this miracle Alavaka realized that his human visitor was no ordinary person who could be scared by a demon. So changing tactics he said to the Buddha: "Is it right that you, a holy man, should enter and sit amongst other's wives when the owner of the house is away?"

At this the Buddha got up to leave the cave-house. And Alavaka thought: "What a fool I am to have wasted my energy trying to frighten this ascetic."

And he asked the Buddha to enter the cave once more. And the Blessed One obeyed. But then again Alavaka told him to leave.

In all, three times each did the demon asked the Buddha to depart and then to enter the cave in the hope of killing him with fatigue.

But, when Alavaka asked the Buddha to leave for a fourth time, the Blessed One refused to comply, saying: “I am not going to obey you, Alavaka. Do whatever you can but I will remain here.”

Unable to force the Buddha to do according to his will, Alavaka again changed his tactic and said: “I will ask you some questions. If you are not able to answer, I will kill you by splitting your heart open and throw your body over to the other side of the river.”

To this, the Blessed One calmly replied: “There is no one, Alavaka, whether man or jinn, who can do such things to me. But if you want to ask anything, you may do so.”

Alavaka was taken aback by this bold reply, but still he proposed to ask the questions which were preserved in his family for many generations.

Asked Alavaka: “What is the greatest wealth for a man? What brings the highest bliss when well mastered? What is the sweetest of all tastes? Which is the best way of life?”

Replied the Buddha: “Faith is the greatest wealth for a man in this world. The ‘Dharma’ when well mastered brings the highest bliss. Truth is the sweetest of all tastes. Wise living is the decent way of life.”

Alavaka asked many more questions, all of which the Blessed one answered to his satisfaction.

And finally, he asked: “Passing from this world to the next, how does one not grieve?”

Replied the Blessed One: "He who possesses these four virtues – truthfulness, good morals, courage and generosity – grieves not after passing away."

Understanding the meaning of the Buddha's words, Alavaka said to himself: "Now I know the secret of my future welfare. It is for my own good that the Buddha came to Alavi."

And he prostrated before the Blessed One and begged to be accepted as a disciple.

The next morning when the officers of Alavi came with the young prince, they were very much surprised to see the Buddha preaching to the demon Alavaka who was listening attentively to his sermon.

And when the boy was handed over to Alavaka, he felt remorse for his past actions and started crying in repentance. Instead of seeing the boy as an offering, he gently stroked the prince on the head, kissed him and handed him back to the officers.

At this, the Buddha blessed the demon and also the young prince. And along with Alavaka, all his wives took the threefold refuge and became lay followers of the Buddha from the jinn community.

And once again prosperity returned to the kingdom of Alavi. People sang praises of the Buddha and many of them accepted his Dharma.

•••

5

Spiritual Powers

Once the Blessed One was dwelling at Veluvana, the bamboo grove near Rajagriha.

At that time, Sariputra and Maha Maudgalyayana were living at the Kapotakandara monastery. And one moonlit night, Sariputra, while sitting with lately shaven head in the open air, fell into a mystical trance.

Now it so happened that two yakshas, who were associates, were travelling from the North Country to the South Country for their business. And when they saw Sariputra in a state of trance, sitting with lately shaven head, the first yaksha said to the second yaksha: "It occurs to me, friend, to give this 'samana' a blow on the head."

But the second yaksha replied: "Enough, friend, do not strike the samana. A renowned man, is this 'samana', very powerful and mighty in spiritual strength."

In all, three times did the first yaksha told of his resolve to strike Sariputra, and each time his friend warned him not to do so.

But ultimately, the first yaksha, not heeding his friend's warning, delivered a blow on the head of Sariputra; such a blow that could have fell an elephant.

But Sariputa was unmoved, drowned in his mystical trance.

And no sooner had the wicked yaksha struck Sariputra, he himself cried out: “I burn, I burn”, and was reduced to ashes. And witnessing it the second yaksha fled in fear.

Now, Maha Maudgalyayana was able to see all of this with the aid of his spiritual eye. And he went to where Sariputra was, and drawing near he said: “I trust, brother, that you are at ease, that you are doing well, that there is no pain.”

By this time Sariputra had come out of his trance, and he heard what Maudgalyayana said. So in reply, he said: “I am at ease, brother Maudgalyayana, and am doing well, but I feel a slight pain in my head.”

“How strange is it, brother Sariputra! How marvelous is it, brother Sariputra! How great is the spiritual power, how great is the might of venerable Sariputra! Just now, brother Sariputra, a certain yaksha delivered a blow on your head and how great was that blow which could have fell an elephant,” said Maudgalyayana in excitement.

Replied Sariputra: “I am at ease, brother Maudgalyayana, I am doing well, but I feel a slight pain in my head. It is strange, brother Maudgalyayana, it is wonderful, brother Maudgalyayana – how great is the spiritual power of the venerable Maudgalyayana, that he saw a yaksha at all. I did not see even a mud-sprite.”

And the Buddha, with the aid of his spiritual ear, was able to hear the far-off conversation that was taking place between his two chief disciples.

And, in this connection, the Blessed One breathed forth this solemn utterance:

"He whose heart, like a rock unshaken stands,

Who is passion free, not angry with the angry,

He whose heart is thus trained,

How shall pain come to such a one?"

• • •

6

Journey To Heaven

It was only seven years after his enlightenment that the Blessed One at the request of his father returned to Kapilavastu.

On the third day, the Buddha was invited to the palace to attend the wedding ceremony of his half-brother Nanda. But before the engagement could take place the Blessed One silently handed his bowl to Nanda, rose and exited. Thinking that the Buddha would take his bowl back, Nanda followed him until they reached the Park of Nyagrodha. There the Blessed One asked his younger brother whether he would like to become a monk. Overawed by the Buddha, Nanda could not but say yes.

But, several years later, Nanda began to regret leaving his wife-to-be, a beautiful girl named Janapada Kalyani. Her last words to him the day he trailed after the Buddha were: "Come back, soon, prince". And Nanda enjoyed no spiritual happiness. His thoughts were constantly directed towards to Janapada Kalyani, and his heart pined for her.

And learning of it, the Buddha used his supernormal powers to take Nanda to a jungle where they saw an ugly little she-monkey who was scalded. And the Blessed One asked Nanda, saying: "Who, Nanda, is more beautiful, the monkey or Janapada Kalyani?"

Nanda naturally replied that there was no comparison between the two and that Janapada Kalyani, reputed to be the most beautiful girl in the land, was by far the most desirable.

The Buddha then once again used his supernormal powers to take Nanda to the heaven where they saw the 'apsaras' at play. And again the Blessed One asked Nanda, saying: "Who, Nanda, do you consider more beautiful? Those nymphs or Janapada Kalyani?"

"Venerable Sir, Janapada Kalyani looks like the scalded she-monkey, compared to those nymphs," replied Nanda.

"Cheer up, Nanda! I promise that you will join the company of those nymphs if you persist as I bid you and take pleasure in living the Holy Life," said the Blessed One.

So, on returning from his dreamful journey, Nanda dedicated himself to his practice but with the sole objective of winning the celestial nymphs.

Now, when the other monks learned of Nanda's wish, they ridiculed him, and he eventually saw his motive as base. So renouncing desire he practiced diligently and soon was able to attain arahantship.

And the very night on which Nanda became an arahant, certain angels of dazzling beauty, illuminating the whole of the Jetavana with their radiance, descended where the Blessed One was, and after paying reverence to the Buddha they informed him of the emancipated condition of Nanda.

The next morning Nanda came to the Blessed One, and after paying his obeisance to the Buddha he sat down respectfully to one side. Being extremely delighted on realizing the exquisite happiness of Nirvana, Nanda thanked the Blessed One, saying: "Lord, I release you from your promise of celestial bliss."

To this, the Blessed One replied: "Since, Nanda, your heart is freed from 'attachment' and the sins, I too am released from that promise."

And the Blessed One, in this connection, breathed forth this solemn utterance:

"He who has crossed the slough of impurity,

Who has crushed the thorns of desire,

The monk, whether there be ease or discomfort,

Is at peace."

•••

7

Heavenly Bliss

Once the Blessed One was dwelling at Sravasti in the Jetavana, the garden of Anathapindika.

At that time, there was a certain Brahmin, a religious man fond in his affections but without deep wisdom. He had a son of great promise, who, when seven years old, was struck with a fatal disease and died. The unfortunate father was unable to control himself; he threw himself upon the corpse and lay there as one dead. The relatives came and buried the dead child. And when the father came to himself, he was so immoderate in his grief that he behaved like an insane person. He no longer gave way to tears but wandered about asking for the residence of Yamaraja, the King of Death, humbly to beg him that his child might be allowed to return to life.

Having arrived at a great Brahmin temple the distraught father went through certain religious rites, and after which he fell asleep and had a vivid dream.

While wandering in his dream he came to a deep mountain pass where he met a number of ascetics who had acquired supreme wisdom.

"Kind Sirs," he said, "Can you tell me where the residence

of Yamaraja is?"

And they asked him: "Good friend, why do you want to know?"

Whereupon he told them his sad story and explained his intentions. Pitying his self-delusion, the ascetics said: "No mortal man can reach the place where Yama dwells, but some four hundred miles westward lies a great city in which many good souls live; every eighth day of the month Yama visits the place, and there may you see him who is the King of Death and ask him for a boon."

The Brahmin rejoicing at the news went to the city and found it as the ascetics had told him. He was admitted to the dread presence of Yama, the King of Death, who, on hearing his request, said: "Your son now lives in the eastern garden where he is disporting himself; go there and ask him to follow you."

Said the happy father: "How does it happen that my son, without having performed one good work, is now living in paradise?"

Replied Yamaraja: "He has obtained celestial happiness not by performing good deeds, but because he died in faith and in love to the Blessed Master, the glorious Buddha."

The delighted father hastened to the garden and saw his beloved child playing with other children, all transfigured by the peace of the blissful existence of a heavenly life. He rushed towards his boy and cried with tears running down his cheeks: "My son, my son, do you not remember me, your father, who watched over you with loving care and tended you in sickness? Return home with me to the land of the living."

But the boy, while struggling to go back to his playmates, upbraided him for using such strange expressions as father and son. "In my present state," he said, "I know no such words, for I am free from delusion."

Taken aback by his son's reply, the Brahmin hopelessly departed, and when he woke from his dream he bethought himself of the Blessed Master, the great Buddha, and resolved to go to him, lay bare his grief, and seek consolation.

Having arrived at the Jetavana the Brahmin told his story to the Buddha and how the boy refused to recognize him. The Blessed One explained to him that worldly relations do not matter much in the heaven, and then, finally, said: "A wise man, understanding the transiency of worldly relations, destroys the cause of grief and escapes from the seething whirlpool of sorrow. Religious wisdom lifts a man above the pleasures and pains of the world and gives him peace everlasting."

When the Buddha had thus spoken, truth dawned on the distraught father and he asked for permission of the Blessed One to enter the community of monks, so as to acquire the heavenly wisdom which alone can give comfort to an afflicted heart.

•••

8

Tale Of A Bandit

Once the Blessed One was staying at Sravasti in the Jetavana, the garden of Anathapindika.

At that time, there was in the realm of Prasenajit, king of Kosala, a robber named Angulimala, a ruffian whose hands were red with blood and was always killing and wounding, and showed no mercy to any living creature. From every human he slew, he took a finger to make for himself a necklace, and so got his name of 'Angulimala', that is, 'Necklace of Fingers'.

With the passage of time things had gotten so worse that people would no longer travel on the road through the forest where Angulimala lay in wait. The upset people started complaining to their king, whilst requesting him to lead his army into the forest and hunt down the serial killer.

The Buddha also felt pain on seeing the suffering of the masses and decided to intervene.

So one day, after having his meal, he took his bowl and outer robe and headed straight to the forest where Angulimala had made his lair.

On the way the cowherds, shepherds, and ploughmen warned him of the danger ahead and advised him to go back if he cared for his life. But the Blessed One didn't heed the warnings and silently passed by on his way into the forest.

And as he walked through the jungle, all of a sudden, he heard a loud voice asking him to stop. The Blessed One turned and saw Angulimala running ferociously towards him with a dagger in his hand, but unfazed he continued to walk. Although Angulimala was running as fast as he could, he was not able to catch up with the Buddha who was walking at a mediocre speed in a dignified manner. This miracle bewildered Angulimala so much that he stopped and pleaded with the Buddha, saying: "Stop, Recluse! Stop!"

At this, the Blessed One said: "I have stopped, Angulimala, you stop too."

Hearing it, Angulimala was still more confused as he himself had stopped but the Buddha was still walking, and so he asked for further explanation.

And the Blessed One said: "I don't kill or harm any living being, so I have stopped. But you still kill living beings, so you haven't stopped yet."

Angulimala was so overcome by the words of the Buddha that he felt remorse for his past actions. He threw away his dagger, tore the garland of fingers, and threw himself at the feet of the Blessed One, pleading with him to keep him in his company.

The Blessed One granted his wish and extended to him the

earliest form of invitation to join the monastic Sangha, saying: "Come, monk."

And then the Buddha led him to the Jeta Grove Monastery where he was staying.

In the meantime, King Prasenajit readied his chosen soldiers with the sole mission of hunting down Angulimala.

In the middle of the day, he drove out of Sravasti with a cavalry of five hundred men heading towards the forest. He drove thus as far as the road was passable for carriages, and then he dismounted from his carriage and went forward on foot to the Jetavana in order to take the blessing of the Buddha before continuing on with his mission.

So he approached the Blessed One, and after paying his obeisance to the Blessed One he sat down respectfully to one side. On being asked by the Buddha the purpose of his visit, the king told him everything.

And the Blessed One said: "Tell me, O King, how would you react if you were to discover that Angulimala has given up his cruel way of living and, instead, has become a monk?"

Replied the king: "O Blessed One, if it were really so as you are saying, I will spare his life, pay reverence to him, and provide him in his monastic vocation."

The Buddha then revealed Angulimala to the king, as he sat only a few feet away with a shaven head. Seeing the dreaded bandit, the king was astounded, at first, but then came back to himself and offered to donate robe materials and other requisites to him. But Angulimala humbly declined the offer by saying that he was happy in the cast-off rags.

Having profound respect for the Buddha, the king trusted his judgement that Angulimala has really changed, and so he rose from his seat, paid homage to the Blessed One, and then departed keeping him on his right.

One day, while wandering door-to-door for alms in Sravasti, Angulimala came across a young woman undergoing a difficult labor. He was deeply moved on seeing the woman's plight and hurried back to the Jetavana. After reporting the matter to the Buddha, Angulimlala asked him what he could do to ease her pain.

And the Blessed One said: "In that case, Angulimala, go into Sravasti and say to that woman: 'Sister, since I was born, I do not recall that I have ever intentionally deprived a living being of life. By this truth, may you be well and may your infant be well!'"

To this, Angulimala replied: "Venerable Sir, wouldn't I be telling a deliberate lie, for I have intentionally deprived many living beings of life."

"Then, Angulimala, go into Sravasti, and say to that woman: 'Sister, since I was born with the noble birth, I do not recall that I have ever intentionally deprived a living being of life. By this truth, may you be well and may your infant be well!'"

“Very good, Venerable Sir,” replied Angulimala, and he hurried back to the woman’s house in Sravasti.

And only when he had delivered the benediction that the woman safely gave birth to her child without feeling any severe pain.

Feeling happy and delighted at being able to help someone, Angulimala reported back to the Buddha whilst praising him.

This event helped Angulimala focus his mind on his basic meditation subject as prior to this there would always appear in his mind’s eye the place in the jungle where he had slain so many innocent people.

After Angulimala had performed the Act of Truth, he was seen to bring safety to people and the people also started to approach him and provide him with alms-food. At last, his earlier name ‘Ahimsaka’, meaning non-violent, fully befitted him.

Most of the people had gained full confidence in his inner transformation and there was no lack of support for him. However, a resentful few could not forget that he was responsible for the deaths of their loved ones. Unable to win revenge through the law, they decided to take matters into their own hands.

One day, when Angulimala was on his alms round, the resentful people attacked him with sticks and stones, and grievously injured him.

With a bleeding head, torn outer robe and a broken alms-bowl, Angulimala somehow managed to return to the monastery.

The Buddha saw him coming in the distance in a dilapidated condition and it took him no time to understand the whole matter. When Angulimala came nearer, the Blessed One said: “Bear it, Brahmin! Bear it! You are experiencing here and now the result of your evil deeds because of which you might have been tortured in hell for many years, for many hundreds of years, for many thousands of years.”

The Buddha’s encouragement helped Angulimala to remain firm and invulnerable in mind and heart, though his body remained exposed to the effects of his former deeds. He endured the ill treatment meted out to him with great patience and eventually became an arahant.

He spent the latter part of his life as a hermit living in the wilderness apart from others except for the rainy season retreats.

Living thus, Angulimala was able to experience the peace of Nirvana, and he once again became famous but this time as a saint.

...

9

The Golden Statue

One of the Buddha's famous disciples was Maha Kashyapa, who grew up in a Brahmin family living in a nearby village of Rajagriha. His original name was Pipphali.

Pipphali's father was very rich and owned a large estate. Despite growing up in luxury, Pipphali found no satisfaction in worldly pleasures. He wished to renounce the world and live the simple life of an ascetic. But his parents were very well aware of his intention, and they pressured him to get married. Being an obedient son, he couldn't go against his parents' wishes. However, he commissioned an artist to caste a golden statue based on his idea of a perfectly beautiful woman. And he demanded that the woman his parents would choose must look exactly like the statue, otherwise he would not marry.

Of course, he never imagined that his parents would be able to find the woman matching the statue, but much to his dismay, they succeeded. With no option left, Pipphali had to marry the statue that came to life in the form of Bhadra Kapilani, a pious and devout lady.

And they ended up being a good match for each other due to their shared beliefs.

Not long after Pipphali's parents passed away and he inherited their estate, the couple mutually agreed that the time had finally come for both of them to leave the family life and become homeless wanderers seeking the Ultimate Truth.

And so that it would not cause a scandal, they both agreed to part company and take different roads.

Bhadra Kapilani ended up going to Sravasti. There she stayed for a number of years with an order of non-Buddhist nuns near the Jetavana. And after the establishment of the Buddhist order of nuns, she became a disciple of the Buddha and joined his Sangha. Soon after, she attained the stage of arahantship and became well known for her patience and compassion. She also became a popular teacher of the Dharma.

And Pipphali ended up meeting the Buddha on the road outside Rajagriha. The Blessed One was sitting beneath a banyan tree, emitting rays of light. And Pipphali was able recognize all the signs and marks of a great man on him. He immediately went up to the Buddha, and after paying reverential salutation to the Blessed One he begged to be accepted as a disciple. After enquiring about his background, the Buddha gave him a brief teaching and then accepted him as a disciple. As a mark of respect for his Master, Pipphali folded his outer robe and gave it to the Buddha to use it as a seat. And when the Buddha remarked upon the softness of the robe, Pipphali requested him to keep it with him. In return, the Blessed One offered his own ragged robe which Pipphali joyfully accepted.

On the advice of the Buddha, Pipphali took up austere ascetic practices and was able to attain arahantship in a short time. He eventually came to be known as the foremost in ascetic discipline, and was given the title of 'Maha Kashyapa', that is, 'Great One of the Kashyapa Clan'.

•••

10

Beauty And Fame

Once the Blessed One was dwelling at Vesali in the mango grove belonging to the famed and beautiful courtesan Amrapali.

Amrapali was fondly known as "nagarvadhu", that is, "bride of the city". The story is that a gardener found her abandoned in the mango grove and raised her as his own daughter. And he named her "Amrapali", that is, "Mango-Guardian". As a young woman she was so beautiful that the Licchavi princes fought each other for her hand in marriage. And finally, to preserve peace, it was decided that she would become the "bride of the city". The position was something like a combination of high-class courtesan and unofficial queen. She became the mistress of the Licchavi princes and of the neighboring royalty who would come visiting her with costly gifts. She became quite wealthy as a result, and was known for her charity and good counsel.

Now, when Amrapali heard that the Buddha was staying in her mango grove, she took her best carriage and drove out to meet him. On arriving at the mango grove, she greeted the Buddha with all proper courtesies and then sat down to hear his teaching. And she was so inspired and uplifted by the Buddha's talk that she invited the Buddha and his Sangha to eat their meal at her place the next morning. The Blessed One consented by his silence and Amrapali took leave of him.

She was in such a haste to get home and make preparations that she almost ran into the Licchavi princes in their chariots, all dressed in red, white, blue, and yellow with make-up to match. They were on their way to pay respects to the Buddha. And Amrapali met the young Licchavis axle to axle, wheel to wheel, yoke to yoke. Taken aback by this attitude of hers, the princes said: "Amrapali, why do you drive up against us like that?"

"Because, young sirs, the Blessed Lord has been invited by me for a meal with his order of monks."

"Amrapali, give us this meal for a hundred thousand pieces!"

"Young sirs, if you were to give me all of Vesali with its revenues, I would not give up such an important meal."

And the Licchavis snapped their fingers, saying: "We have been outdone by the mango-woman!"

They then proceeded on with their journey to Amrapali's mango grove where the Blessed One was dwelling. And having arrived there they paid ther reverence to the Buddha and sat down to hear his teaching. They too were inspired and uplifted by the Buddha's talk, and they then invited the Buddha to eat with them the next morning. But the Blessed One informed them that he had already accepted

Amrapali's invitation. And once again the Licchavis snapped their fingers and bemoaned the fact that Amrapali had beaten them.

The next day, the Buddha and his Sangha ate their meal at Amrapali's place. And when the meal was over the Buddha gave her further instruction in the Dharma. As a result, her faith in the Buddha increased evermore. And she donated her mango grove to the Sangha.

When Amrapali grew old, she retired from the worldly life and became a nun. Through contemplating the loss of her beauty in old age, as well as the fame, wealth and prestige it had brought, she realized that all phenomena are marked by impermanence and suffering. She devoutly followed the Dharma and diligently practiced the meditation, and was able to attain arahantship and experience the peace of Nirvana in her lifetime.

•••

11

Kindliness And Love

Once Ananda was sent on some errand by the Buddha on a hot summer day. While still on his way Ananda felt thirsty. On noticing a well near a village, he approached it and saw a maiden filling her buckets. Her name was Pakati and she belonged to the Matanga caste.

And when Ananda asked her for water to drink, she replied: "O Brahmin, I am too humble and mean to give you water to drink, do not ask any service of me lest your holiness be contaminated, for I am of low caste."

Said Ananda: "I ask not for caste but for water."

Hearing it, the Matanga girl's heart leaped joyfully, and she gave Ananda to drink.

After quenching his thirst, Ananda thanked her and went on his way; but she followed him from a distance. And coming to know that Ananda was a disciple of Shakyamuni, the girl repaired to the Buddha and cried out: "O Lord, help me, and let me live in the place where your disciple Ananda dwells, so that I may see him and minister unto him, for I love Ananda."

Perceiving her emotions, the Blessed One said: "Pakati, your heart is full of love but you haven't understood your own sentiments. It is not Ananda that you love, but his kindness."

Outwitted by the Buddha, Pakati could not but nod in approval.

"Accept, then," continued the Blessed One, "the kindness you have seen him practice unto you, and in the humility of your station practice it unto others.

"Verily, there is great merit in the generosity of a king when he is kind to a slave; but there is greater merit in the slave when he ignores the wrongs which he suffers and cherishes kindness and good-will to all mankind. He will cease to hate his oppressors, and even when powerless to resist their usurpation will with compassion pity their arrogance and supercilious demeanor.

"Blessed are you, Pakati, for though you are a Matanga you can be a model for noble men and noble women. You are of low caste, but Brahmins may learn a lesson from you. Swerve not from the path of justice and righteousness, and you will outshine the royal glory of queens on the throne."

Pakati understood the words of the Blessed One, and took the threefold refuge and went away.

•••

12

Charms And Desire

Vasavadatta was a courtesan in Mathura. Once she happened to see Upagutta, one of the Buddha's disciples, a tall and handsome youth, and fell desperately in love with him. She sent an invitation to the young man, but he replied: "The time has not yet arrived when Upagutta will visit Vasavadatta."

The courtesan was surprised with his reply, and she sent again for him, saying: "Vasavadatta desires love, not gold, from Upagutta."

But, yet again, he made the same enigmatic reply and did not come.

A few months later Vasavadatta was having a love intrigue with the chief of the artisans. But, at this time, a wealthy merchant came to Mathura, and fell in love with Vasavadatta.

Greedy for his wealth and fearing the jealousy of her other lover, she contrived the death of the chief of the artisans, and concealed his body under a dung-hill.

When the chief of the artisans went missing, his friends and relatives searched for him and found his body.

Vasavadatta was tried by a judge who declared her guilty, and condemned to have her ears, nose, hands and feet cut off, and flung her into a graveyard.

Vasavadatta had been a passionate girl, but kind to her servants, and one of her maids followed her, and out of love for her former mistress ministered to her in her agonies, and chased away the crows.

Now, at this time, Upaguttta decided to visit Vasavadatta.

When she saw him coming in the distance, she ordered her maid to collect and hide under a cloth her severed limbs.

On approaching, Upaguttta greeted her respectfully, but Vasavadatta said with petulance: "Once the body was fragrant like the lotus, and I offered you my love. In those days I was covered with pearls and fine muslin. Now I am mangled by the executioner and covered with filth and blood."

"Sister," said the young man, "it is not for my pleasure that I approach you. It is to restore to you a nobler beauty than the charms which you have lost.

"The charms of a lovely form are treacherous, and quickly lead into temptations, which have proved too strong for you. But there is a beauty that will not fade, and if you will listen to the doctrine of our Lord, the Buddha, you will find that peace which you haven't found in the restless world of sinful pleasures."

On hearing the talk on Dharma, Vasavadatta became calm and a spiritual happiness soothed the tortures of her bodily pain; for when there is much suffering there is also great bliss.

And after having taken the threefold refuge, she died in pious submission to the punishment of her crime.

•••

13

The Mustard Seed

Kisa Gotami was the wife of a wealthy man of Sravasti. She had an only son, and he died. And she became desperate to revive him. In her grief she carried the dead child to all her neighbours, asking them for medicine to cure the child.

And the people said: "She has lost her senses. The boy is dead."

At length, Kisa Gotami met an old man who heeded her request, saying: "I cannot give you medicine for your child, but I know a physician who can."

With a glimpse of hope, the distraught mother asked, saying: "Pray tell me, Sir; who is it?"

"Go to Shakyamuni, the Buddha who dwells at Jetavana," replied the kind-hearted man.

And Kisa Gotami hurried to the Jeta Grove Monastery, and on arriving there she found the Buddha in the middle of a discourse.

And she cried out: "Lord, give me the medicine that will cure my boy."

The Blessed One stopped his discourse and noticed that the boy was dead. Seeing the distraught condition of the mother, he said: “I want a handful of mustard seed.”

And when the lady in her joy promised to procure it, the Buddha added: “The mustard seed should be taken from a house where no one has lost a child, husband, parent or any relative.”

Poor Kisa Gotami now went from house to house, and the people pitied her, saying: “Here is mustard seed; take it!” But when she asked, “Did a son or daughter, a father or mother, die in your family?” the householders answered, “Alas the living are few, but the dead are many. Do not remind us of our deepest grief.”

And there was no house but some beloved one had died in it.

After Kisa Gotami had done many a round she became tired and hopeless, and sat down at the wayside, watching the lights of the city, as they flickered up and extinguished again.

At last the darkness of the night reigned everywhere.

Now she considered the fate of humans, that how their lives flicker up and then are extinguished. And, at this moment, truth dawned on her and she said to herself: “How selfish am I in my grief! Death is common to all; yet in this valley of desolation there is a path that leads one, who has surrendered all selfishness, to immortality.”

And with this thought she put away the selfishness of her

affection for her child, and had the lifeless body buried in the forest.

Then she returned to the Buddha who comforted her with kind words, and then preached to her the doctrine of truth. And as a result, she became a stream-enterer and took the threefold refuge.

• • •

14

Life And Water

Once when the Buddha was staying at the Nyagrodha Park near Kapilavastu, a serious dispute broke out between the Shakyas and Koliyas.

They had directed the Rohini River to be constricted between the city of Kapilavastu and Devadaha for irrigation of their fields on its bank. In a certain month when the crops started to whither and the river ran low, labourers and residents of both the cities assembled for a meeting. The Koliyas remarked that if the water continued to be shared by both sides, it would be inadequate for both clans. And since their crops could ripen with one more watering, they should have it. To that, the Shakyas rebutted that after the Koliyas have stocked their storehouses, they the Shakyas would not be willing to take their precious minerals, gems and money to visit them door to door in exchange for food. They too insisted that as their crops could ripen with one more watering, they should have the water. Thus began their bickering, out of mutual reluctance to let the water be taken by the other. And they began to abuse each other in filthy language. When things got more bitter one man struck another, with the other man retaliating, sparking off a fight. To add fuel to the fire was the casting of aspersions on each other's royal lineage.

Both sides reported the quarrel to their ministers who reported it to their royal households. And the leaders of the respective clans also got infuriated and decided to wage a war on each other.

Armed for battle, the Shakyas and Koliyas declared to show their strength and power to each other.

When the Buddha learned of the impending battle, he immediately used his supernormal power to levitate through the air where the conflict was and sat cross-legged in the air above the middle of the Rohini River to catch everyone's attention.

The Shakyas and Koliyas on seeing this amazing miracle threw off their weapons and paid homage to the Blessed One.

But when the Buddha enquired on the origin of the quarrel, the kings of both sides expressed their ignorance. He then asked who would be likely to know the exact cause. When the army's chief commander was directed to, he replied that the viceroy would be likely to know. This went on and on until the labourers were questioned, who replied that the quarrel began over not sharing the water.

The Blessed One then asked the leaders, saying: "Tell me, O Kings, how much the water is worth?"

"Very little, of course," came the reply.

"And how much the human lives are worth?"

"Beyond price," replied the kings.

Then the Buddha asked, saying: "Is it fitting, O Kings, that for very little water one should destroy human lives which are beyond price?"

And to this all became silent. The Buddha then asked both the sides to reflect on their actions, saying that if he were not there they would have let flow a river of blood out of their evil desires.

And the Blessed One, on this occasion, breathed forth this solemn utterance:

"We live indeed so happily,

Unhating amidst haters;

Among those who are hateful,

We dwell free from hate."

•••

15

The Sower

Bharadvaja, a wealthy Brahmin farmer, was celebrating his harvest-thanksgiving when the Blessed One came wandering while on his alms round.

Some of the people paid him reverence, but the Brahmin angrily said: "O Samana, it would be more fitting for you to go to work than to beg. Just see me. I plough and sow, and having ploughed and sown, I eat. If you would do likewise, you, too, would have something to eat."

The Blessed One answered, saying: "O Brahmin, I, too, plough and sow, and having ploughed and sown, I eat."

"Do you profess to be a husbandman?" asked the Brahmin, "Where, then, are your bullocks? Where are the seeds and the plough?"

The Blessed One replied: "Faith is the seed I sow; good works are the rain that fertilizes it; wisdom and modesty are the plough; my mind is the guiding-rein; I lay hold of the handle of the law; earnestness is the goad I use, and exertion is my draught-ox. This ploughing is ploughed to destroy the weeds of illusion. The harvest it yields is the immortal fruit of Nirvana, and thus all sorrow ends."

The Brahmin was left highly impressed by the Buddha's talk, and he poured rice-milk into a golden bowl and offered it to the Blessed One, saying: "Let the Teacher of mankind partake of the rice-milk, for the venerable Gautama ploughs a ploughing that bears the fruit of immortality."

•••

16

The Greedy Listener

Anathapindika, the wealthy merchant of Sravasti, was a devout follower of the Buddha but his son Kala was not. And Anathapindika was very much worried about his wayward son.

Kala never showed any desire to visit the Buddha, or to see him when he came to his father's house or to hear the Dharma, or to perform services for the Order. Moreover, whenever his father said to him, "Dear son, do not do this", he paid no attention to what his father said.

Now, Anathapindika thought that if his son continued like this he would certainly go to hell after death. So thinking of a plan he said to his son: "Dear son, take upon yourself the precepts of Uposatha Day, go to the monastery, listen to the Dharma, and then return. If you will do so, I will give you a hundred pieces of money."

"Will you really give me this, dear father?" asked the greedy son.

"That I will, dear son," replied the father.

And after he had made his father repeat his promise three times, Kala took upon himself the precepts of Uposatha Day and went to the monastery. But not caring to listen to the Dharma, he lay down to sleep in a pleasant place and returned home early in the morning.

Thereupon his father said: "My son has undertaken the precepts of Uposatha Day; bring him rice-porridge and other food straightaway."

Thus saying, the father caused food to be brought and given to him. But Kala said: "Unless I receive the money, I will not eat."

So saying he steadfastly refused whatever was brought to him. His father, who could not endure forcing his son to eat, ordered that the money be presented to him.

The greedy son first took the purse of money into his hands and then ate the food that was brought to him.

On the following day the father sent him forth, saying to him: "Dear son, I will give you a thousand pieces of money if you will stand before the Blessed One, learn a single verse of the Dharma, and then return to me."

In his greed for money, Kala went to the monastery and took his stand before the Buddha. But no sooner had he heard a single verse that he desired to run away. So he couldn't grasp the meaning of the verse.

Kala thought that he wouldn't get the thousand pieces of money until and unless he was able to fully explain the verse to his father. So he remained there listening to the talk of the Buddha.

Kala listened to the Dharma with a firm resolution to learn, and finally he was able to grasp the meaning. Such was the effect of the Buddha's teaching that Kala was established in the fruit of stream-entry.

On the following day he accompanied the Order of monks presided over by the Buddha to Sravasti.

Actually, the Buddha and his Sangha were invited by Kala's father for a feast on that day. And when Anathapindika saw Kala, he said to himself: "Today the demeanor of my son pleases me."

But, on the other hand, his son thought: "I hope my father will not give me the money today in the presence of the Buddha. I hope he will conceal the fact that it was for the sake of money that I took upon myself the precepts of the Uposatha Day."

When the Buddha and his monks were comfortably seated, Anathapindika served them rice-porridge and other delicacies.

And when the feast was over, Anathapindika placed the purse containing a thousand pieces of money before his son and said: "Dear son, you will remember that I promised to give you a thousand pieces of money if you were to go to the monastery. Here is the promised amount. Take it."

But Kala was deeply embarrassed to see the money presented to him in the very presence of the Buddha, and he said: "I do not care for the money."

"Take the money, dear son," requested the father.

But Kala refused to touch it. And Anathapindika said to the Blessed One: “Reverend Sir, today the demeanor of my son pleases me.”

“And how is that, Anathapindika?” asked the Blessed One.

“The day before yesterday I sent him to the monastery, saying to him, ‘I will give you a hundred pieces of money’; yesterday, he refused to eat because I did not give him the money, but today, when I give him the money, he refuses to touch it.”

“It is even so, Anathapindika. Today, in attaining the fruit of stream-entry, your son has attained that which surpasses the attainment of a Universal Monarch.”

And thus the plan of Anathapindika paid off. He was very much relieved to see his son on the right path and more importantly under the guidance of the right teacher.

•••

17

The Disobedient Elephant

As a young boy the conduct of Rahula was not always marked by a love of truth, and so the Blessed One sent him to a distant monastery to govern his mind and to govern his tongue.

After some time the Buddha repaired to the place, and Rahula was filled with joy. The Blessed One ordered his son to bring him a basin of water and to wash his feet, to which Rahula obeyed.

When Rahula had washed his father's feet, the Blessed One asked him, saying: "Is the water now fit for drinking?"

"No, my lord," replied Rahula, "the water is defiled."

Said the Blessed One: "Now consider your own case, Rahula. Although you are my son, although you are a samana who has voluntarily given up everything, you are unable to guard your tongue from untruth; and thus defiled your mind."

And when the water had been poured away, the Buddha asked again, saying: "Is this vessel now fit for holding water to drink?"

"No, my lord," replied Rahula, "the vessel, too, has become unclean."

"Now consider your own case, Rahula. Although you wear the yellow robe, are you fit for any high purpose when you have become unclean like the vessel?"

Then the Blessed One lifting up the empty basin and whirling it round asked Rahula, saying: "Are you not afraid lest it shall fall and break?"

"No, my lord," replied Rahula, "it is cheap, its loss will not amount to much."

"Now consider your own case, Rahula," said the Blessed One, "your mind is whirled about in endless thoughts, and as your body is made of the same substance as other material things that will crumble to dust, there is no loss if it to be broken. He who is given to speaking untruths is an object of contempt to the wise."

Hearing it, Rahula was filled with shame, and the Blessed One addressed him once more and said:

"Listen and I will tell you a parable. There was a king who had a very powerful elephant, able to cope with five hundred ordinary elephants. When going to war, the elephant was armed with sharp swords on his tusks, with scythes on his shoulders, spears on his feet, and an iron ball at his tail. The elephant-master rejoiced on seeing the noble creature so well equipped, and knowing that a slight wound by an arrow in the trunk would be fatal, he had taught the elephant to keep his trunk well coiled up. But during the battle the elephant stretched forth his trunk to seize a sword. His master was frightened and consulted with the king, and they decided that the elephant was no longer fit to be used in battle.

"O Rahula! If men would only guard their tongues all would be well. Be like the fighting elephant who guards his trunk against the arrow that strikes in the center. By love of truth the sincere escape iniquity. Like the elephant well subdued and quiet, who permits the king to mount on his trunk, thus the man that reveres righteousness will endure faithfully throughout his life."

Rahula, on hearing these words, was filled with deep sorrow; he never again gave any occasion for complaint, and forthwith he sanctified his life by earnest exertions.

And in his lifetime he was able to attain arahantship and experience the peace of Nirvana.

• • •

18

Evil Befalls The Evil-Doer

Once the Buddha was dwelling at the Ghosita Monastery near Kosambi.

At that time, Udena was the king of Kosambi and Samavati was one of his queens. Samavati had five hundred maids-of-honor staying with her at the palace; she also had a maid-servant called Khujjuttara. Every day the maid had to buy flowers for the queen from the florist Sumana. On one occasion Khujjuttara had the opportunity to listen to a religious discourse delivered by the Buddha at the home of Sumana, and consequently she attained stream-entry.

On returning to the palace she repeated the discourse of the Buddha to Samavati and the five hundred maids of honor, and as a result they also attained stream-entry.

And from that day Khujjuttara did not have to do any menial work, but took the place of mother and teacher to Samavati. She listened to the discourses of the Buddha and repeated them to the queen and her maids.

Samavati and her maids wished very much to see the Buddha and pay their obeisance to him, but were afraid that the king might be displeased with them. So, making holes in the walls of the palace, they looked through them and paid obeisance to the Buddha whenever he passed by.

At this time, King Udena had another queen by the name of Magandiya. And she bore a deep grudge against the Buddha as he had once rejected her marriage proposal presented to him by her father.

Now, Magandiya came to know of the arrival of the Buddha in Kosambi, and how Samavati and her maids paid obeisance to him through holes in the walls of their living quarters. And she thought of a plan to take her revenge on the Buddha and also to harm Samavati.

So, accordingly, she told the king that Samavati had outside contacts and was being disloyal to the king, and the proof to which was the presence of holes in her living quarter.

King Udena inspected the holes in the walls and asked for explanation from Samavati. But when the truth was told he didn't get angry.

Despite her failure, Magandiya never gave up but kept on trying to make the king believe that Samavati was not loyal to him and was trying to kill him.

On one occasion, knowing that the king would be visiting Samavati in a few hours and that he would be taking along his lute with him, Magandiya inserted a snake into the lute and closed its hole with a bunch of flowers. And then she followed the king to Samavati's quarters after trying to stop him on the pretext that she had some presentiment and felt worried about his safety.

On reaching there, Magandiya cleverly removed the bunch

of flowers from the mouth of the lute without herself getting noticed, and then she quietly went away. The snake came out hissing and coiled itself on the bed. When the king saw the snake, he believed Magandiya's words that Samavati was really trying to eliminate him. And he became furious and commanded Samavati to stand at a distance and all her ladies to line up behind her. Then he fitted his bow with an arrow dipped in poison and aiming precisely at Samavati he shot the arrow.

But Samavati and her ladies bore no ill-will towards the king and remained firm in their faith. And to everyone's surprise, the arrow rebounded from her without doing any harm, although an arrow shot by the king usually went even through a rock.

This miracle made the king realize the innocence of Samavati, and he gave her permission to invite the Buddha and his monks for alms-food and for religious discourses.

Magandiya, realizing that none of her plans had materialized, made a final infallible plan. She sent a message to her uncle with full instructions to go to Samavati's palace and burn down the building with all the women inside.

And the uncle with the help of some his relatives acted likewise, secretly in the darkness of the night, without getting noticed by any of the guards.

While their apartments were burning, Samavati and her maids with a firm faith kept on meditating, and thus they were martyred in the way of Dharma.

As the news of the fire spread, the king and his men rushed to the scene but it was too late for them to do anything. And the king was immensely grieved at his loss.

He suspected that it was done at the instigation of Magandiya, but he hid his suspicion and, instead, said to her: "While Samavati was alive, I had been fearful and alert thinking I might be harmed by her; only now, my mind is at peace. Who could have done this? It must have been done only by someone who loves me dearly!"

Unable to control herself at the charming words of the king, Magandiya promptly admitted that it was she who had instructed her uncle to do it. Whereupon the king pretended to be very pleased with her and said that he would do her a great favor and honor all her relatives who were involved in this deed.

And unsuspecting, Magandiya summoned her relatives, and gladly they came expecting a reward.

But, on their arrival, all of them including Magandiya were seized and burnt in the palace courtyard by the order of the king.

Soon the news of these two incidents spread throughout Kosambi, and the Buddha and his monks also came to know about it.

And the Blessed One, in this connection, breathed forth this solemn utterance:

"One who is mindful like Samavati,
is truly alive even though physically dead;
But one who is negligent like Magandiya,
is as good as dead even while living."

•••

19

Truth Alone Triumphs

Once the Blessed One was dwelling at Sravasti in the Jetavana, the garden of Anathapindika.

At that time, the Buddha and his Sangha of monks were held in reverence but the wandering monks of the heretical sects were not. And those wandering monks of the heretical sects could not endure the honor extended to the Blessed One and his Sangha.

So they thought of a plan and went to where the wandering nun Sundari was, and said to her: "Is it in your power, sister, to do something for your relatives?"

"What I am to do, sirs, what is it in my power to do? I am ready to sacrifice my life for my relatives," replied Sundari.

"Then go at once, sister, to the Jetavana," advised the wicked monks.

"Be it so, sirs," said Sundari, and, unsuspecting, she directed her steps towards the Jeta Grove Monastery.

And these wandering monks of the heretical sects followed her secretly, and on arriving at an isolated place they deprived her of her life and threw her body into a ruined well in the Jetavana.

They then went to the palace and complained to the king about the disappearance of the wandering nun Sundari, and also hinted that something might have happened to her in the Jetavana. And the king sent some of his men with them to search the Jeta Grove Monastery.

After a brief search the monks of the heretical sects took out the lifeless body of Sundari from the ruined well, placed it on a litter and carried it to the city. And stopping at an intersection of four roads they called out to the people and blamed the Buddhist monks for the death of Sundari.

And as a result, the people of Sravasti began to use harsh and improper language towards the bhikshus, calling out: "Shameless are the Shakya sons, impious, wicked, liars and depraved!"

And the bhikshus were very much depressed by such behaviour and attitude of the people towards them. So they went to where the Blessed One was, and after paying reverence to him they sat down respectfully apart; and while thus sitting they complained to him about the ill-treatment meted out to them by the people of Sravasti.

The Blessed One encouraged them to be patient, uplifted their morale by giving a calm and well-reasoned talk, and then finally said: "This uproar, O Bhikshus, will not last long, it will last for seven days only, and at the end of the seventh day it will subside.

"Therefore, O Bhikshus, reprove those men of Sravasti, who, when they see you, use harsh and improper language, with these verses:

The liar goes to hell, also he

who having done an action, says, 'I have not done it.'

Men of base actions both, on departing

they will share the same destiny in the Hereafter."

So the bhikshus, having learnt by heart these verses in the presence of the Buddha, reproved those men of Sravasti who reviled them during their alms round.

And the people said among themselves: "These bhikshus, these Shakya sons are unreasonable, we have no more to do with them."

Thus the uproar did not last long, for seven days only did it last, and at the end of the seventh day it subsided.

And a number of bhikshus, delighted they were, went to the Buddha praising him for his prediction.

And the Blessed One, in this connection, breathed forth this solemn utterance:

"The unrestrained pierce others with their words,

As one elephant pierces another in battle.

When the Bhikshu, of uncorrupted heart,

Hears the utterance of harsh words,

He bears them with resignation."

•••

20

The Man Born Blind

There was a man born blind, and he said: "I do not believe in the world of light and appearance. There are no colors, bright or somber. There is no sun, no moon, no stars. No one has witnessed these things." His friends remonstrated with him, but he clung to his opinion: "What you say that you see," he objected, "are illusions. If colors existed I should be able to touch them. They have no substance and are not real. Everything real has weight, but I feel no weight where you see colors."

A physician was called to see the blind man. He mixed four simples, and when he applied them to the cataract of the blind man the gray film melted, and his eyes acquired the faculty of sight.

The Tathagata is the physician, the cataract is the illusion of the thought "I am", and the four simples are the four noble truths.

•••

21

The Prodigal Son

There was a householder's son who went away into a distant country, and while the father accumulated immeasurable riches, the son became miserably poor. And the son while searching for food and clothing happened to come to the country in which his father lived. The father saw him in his wretchedness, for he was ragged and brutalized by poverty, and ordered some of his servants to call him. When the son saw the place to which he was conducted, he thought: "I must have evoked the suspicion of a powerful man, and he will throw me into prison." Full of apprehension he made his escape before he had seen his father.

Then the father sent messengers out after his son, who was caught and brought back in spite of his cries and lamentations. Thereupon the father ordered his servants to deal tenderly with his son, and he appointed a laborer of his son's rank and education to employ the lad as a helpmate on the estate. And the son was pleased with his new situation. From the window of his palace the father watched the boy, and when he saw that he was honest and industrious, he promoted him higher and higher.

After some time, he summoned his son and called together

all his servants, and made the secret known to them. Then the poor man was exceedingly glad and he was full of joy at meeting his father. Not only he had found my father but all his property and treasure was now his.

Just so, little by little must the minds of men be trained for higher truths.

•••

22

The Light Of The World

There was a certain Brahmin in Kosambi, a wrangler and well versed in the Vedas. As he found no one whom he regarded his equal in debate he used to carry a lighted torch in his hand, and when asked for the reason of his strange conduct, he replied: “The world is so dark that I carry this torch to light it up, as far as I can.” A samana sitting in the market-place heard these words and said: “My friend, if your eyes are blind to the sight of the omnipresent light of the day, do not call the world dark. Thy torch adds nothing to the glory of the sun and your intention to illumine the minds of others is as futile as it is arrogant.” Whereupon the Brahmin asked: “Where is the sun of which you speak?” And the samana replied: “The wisdom of the Tathagata is the sun of the mind. His radiancy is glorious by day and night, and he whose faith is strong will not lack light on the path to Nirvana where he will inherit bliss everlasting.”

...

23

Luxurious Living

While the Buddha was preaching his doctrine for the conversion of the world in the neighborhood of Sravasti, a man of great wealth who suffered from many ailments came to him with clasped hands and said: "World-honored Buddha, pardon me for my want of respect in not saluting you as I ought but I suffer greatly from obesity, excessive drowsiness, and other complaints, so that I cannot move without pain."

The Tathagata, seeing the luxuries with which the man was surrounded, asked him: "Have you a desire to know the cause of your ailments?" And when the wealthy man expressed his willingness to learn, the Blessed One said: "There are five things which produce the condition of which you complain: opulent dinners, love of sleep, hankering after pleasure, thoughtlessness, and lack of occupation. Exercise self-control at your meals, and take upon yourself some duties that will exercise your abilities and make you useful to your fellow-men. In following this advice you will prolong your life."

The rich man remembered the words of the Buddha and after some time having recovered his lightness of body and youthful buoyancy returned to the World-honored One and, coming afoot without horses and attendants, said to him: “Master, you have cured my bodily ailments; I come now to seek enlightenment of my mind.”

And the Blessed One said: “The worldling nourishes his body, but the wise man nourishes his mind. He who indulges in the satisfaction of his appetites works his own destruction; but he who walks in the path will have both - the salvation from evil and a prolongation of life.”

•••

24

The Listless Fool

There was a rich Brahmin, well advanced in years, who, unmindful of the impermanence of earthly things and anticipating a long life, had built himself a large house. The Buddha wondered why a man so near to death had built a mansion with so many apartments, and he sent Ananda to the rich Brahmin to preach to him the four noble truths and the eightfold path of salvation. The Brahmin showed Ananda his house and explained to him the purpose of its numerous chambers, but to the instruction of the Buddha's teachings he gave no heed. Ananda said: "It is the habit of the fools to say, 'I have children and wealth.' He who says so is not even master of himself; how can he claim possession of children, riches, and servants? Many are the anxieties of the worldly, but they know nothing of the changes of the future."

Scarcely had Ananda left, when the old man was stricken with apoplexy and fell dead. The Buddha said, for the instruction of those who were ready, to learn: "A fool, though he live in the company of the wise, understands nothing of the true doctrine, as a spoon tastes not the flavor of the soup. He thinks of himself only, and unmindful of the advice of good counselors is unable to deliver himself."

•••

25

The Uninstructed Cub

Devadatta, a cousin of the Buddha, though lived the life of an ascetic but was full of hatred and deceit. Through his jealousy of the Buddha he gained nothing of the religious life. He also dared to form a rival Sangha by creating a schism in the Buddha's Sangha.

Once the Blessed One addressed his disciples and starting with a parable, he said:

"Once, monks, there were some elephants living near a big pond in a forest. They would go into the pond and pull up lotus stalks with their trunks, and when they had washed them quite clean, they would chew them up and swallow them free from mud. That was good for both their looks and their health, and they incurred no death or deadly suffering because of that. But some young calves, uninstructed by those elephants, went into the pond and pulled up lotus stalks with their trunks; but instead of washing them quite clean, they chewed them up and swallowed them along with mud. That was not good for either their looks or their health, and they incurred death and deadly suffering because of that.

"So, too, monks, Devadatta will die miserably through imitating me."

•••

26

The Mad Elephant

Once Devadatta hatched a plan to eliminate the Buddha. He went to the royal stable where a huge and fierce elephant named Nalagiri was kept. He approached the mahouts and flaunting his royal patronage managed to convince them in releasing the elephant in the Buddha's path when he would be entering the city on his alms round.

Next day, the Blessed One with his group of monks walked through the streets of Rajagriha to collect alms. And as he turned through a corner into a narrow street, Nalagiri the fierce elephant was set loose.

People ran helter-skelter to get out of its way. The whole atmosphere was filled with shouts and frightening screams, and people looked out of their windows and climbed onto the roofs of the houses to see what would happen next.

The mad elephant charged down the street straight towards the Buddha and his group. Fearing for their lives, the monks moved away except Ananda who stood by his Master.

As the tusker approached the Blessed One, people were filled with fear awaiting something bad to happen. But, to their surprise, the Buddha was able to suffuse the giant with his thoughts of loving-kindness, so much that Nalagiri quietened down allowing the Blessed One to approach him and gently stroke his forehead.

This confrontation caused a sensation in Rajagriha, and for weeks people went around the city singing praises of the Buddha, saying:

"Some are tamed by goads and whips,

But the elephant by the great sage was tamed

By loving-kindness, without sword or stick."

•••

27

The Marriage-Feast In Jambunada

There was a man in Jambunada who was to be married the next day, and he thought: "Would that the Buddha, the Blessed One, might be present at the wedding!" And the Blessed One passed by his house and met him, and when he read the silent wish in the heart of the bridegroom, he consented to enter. When the Holy One appeared with the retinue of his many bhikshus, the host, whose means were limited, received them as best he could, saying: "Eat, my Lord, and all your congregation, according to your desire."

While the holy men ate, the meats and drinks remained undiminished, and the host thought to himself: "How wondrous is this! I should have had plenty for all my relatives and friends. Would that I had invited them all!" When this thought was in the host's mind, all his relatives and friends entered the house; and although the hall in the house was small there was room in it for all of them. They sat down at the table and ate, and there was more than enough for all of them.

The Blessed One was pleased to see so many guests full of good cheer and he quickened them and gladdened them with words of truth, proclaiming the bliss of righteousness:

"The greatest happiness which a mortal man can imagine is

the bond of marriage that ties together two loving hearts. But there is a greater happiness still: it is the embrace of truth. Death will separate husband and wife, but death will never affect him who has espoused the truth. Therefore be married unto the truth and live with the truth in holy wedlock. The husband who loves his wife and desires for a union that shall be everlasting must be faithful to her so as to be like truth itself, and she will rely upon him and revere him and minister unto him. And the wife who loves her husband and desires a union that shall be everlasting must be faithful to him so as to be like truth itself; and he will place his trust in her, he will provide for her. Verily, I say unto you, their children will become like their parents and will bear witness to their happiness. Let no man be single, let everyone be wedded in holy love to the truth. And when Death, the destroyer, comes to separate the visible forms of your being, you will continue to live in the truth, and will partake of the life everlasting, for the truth is immortal."

There was no one among the guests but was strengthened in his, spiritual life, and recognized the sweetness of a life of righteousness; and they took refuge in the Buddha, the Dharma, and the Sangha.

•••

28

In Search Of A Thief

Having sent out his disciples, the Blessed One himself wandered from place to place until he reached Uruvela. On his way he sat down in a grove to rest, and it happened that in that same grove was a party of thirty friends who were enjoying themselves with their wives; and while they were sporting, some of their goods were stolen. Then the whole party went in search of the thief and, meeting the Blessed One sitting under a tree, saluted him and said: "Pray, Lord, did you see the thief pass by with our goods?"

And the Blessed One said: "Which is better for you, that you go in search for the thief or for yourselves?" And the youths cried: "In search for ourselves!"

"Well then," said the Blessed One, "sit down and I will preach the truth to you."

And the whole party sat down and they listened eagerly to the words of the Blessed One. Having grasped the truth, they praised the doctrine and took refuge in the Buddha.

...

29

Aversion To Miracles

Once a householder in Rajagriha erected a long pole in front of his house and placed a precious bowl of sandalwood decorated with jewels on top of it. And he made a proclamation that if a monk of any sect was able to bring the bowl down without using a ladder or a stick with a hook or without climbing the pole, then he could take the precious bowl as a reward for his feat.

At that time, Maha Maudgalyayana along with some fellow monks happened to pass by the pole and they noticed the bowl hung over it, and also learned about the proclamation made by the householder.

As Maha Maudgalyayana was well-known for his supernormal powers, so his fellow monk Pindola urged him to prove the superiority of the Buddha's Sangha by bringing down the bowl.

However, Maudgalyayana refused, saying that Pindola himself possessed sufficient powers to do it.

So Pindola just stretched out his hands and the bowl miraculously landed on his palms. And witnessing this supernormal feat the lay people erupted in joy, and they went to the Buddha praising him and his Sangha of monks, and then told him everything about Pindola's feat.

The Blessed One, of course, was not at all amused to hear all this, and he summoned Pindola with the bowl. And when Pindola came, the Buddha took the precious bowl from him and broke it into pieces. Then he rebuked Pindola by saying that a monk should not display supernormal powers for the sake of impressing the laity.

•••

30

Miracle Of Teaching

Once the Buddha was traveling with his disciples when they arrived at the bed of a river. They sat down patiently awaiting the boat to come so that they could go to the other side. As they were waiting an old sage walked by them and walked over the water onto the other side. The disciples were awe struck and when they were all in the boat they were muttering amongst themselves. Buddha knew what was coming next, when they asked him: "If you are the enlightened one, how is it that you did not walk on the water?"

Buddha smiled at them and responded: "If I had to walk across the water, what would you'll have done. I could have walked over the water but how would that be beneficial to you?"

…

31

A Herd Of Cows

A man had a herd of two hundred and fifty cows and took great care looking after their welfare. One day, however, a tiger ate one of them—and when the man noticed this, he thought: “I’ve lost one of my cows, and my herd is incomplete. What’s the point of having all these other cows?” And with that, the man drove all the cows off a cliff and to their death.

He is like a person who, after breaking just one precept of righteousness, thinks, “I’ve broken one, so I might as well abandon them all.”

•••

32

Converting Inventory

The son of a wealthy man found some valuable aloe wood at the bottom of a river, and took it to sell at the bazaar. However, his price was too high, and he found no buyers. Growing discouraged and desperate, he noticed a nearby charcoal seller doing brisk sales, and he decided to burn his aloe wood into charcoal. He managed to sell the charcoal easily, but the money he got for it was nowhere near the value of the aloe wood.

This is similar to how some people practice diligently at first to achieve spiritual goals, but soon grow discouraged at some obstacle, and choose to abandon great things and give up a great deal in order to accept a trivial amount.

•••

33

The King's Decree

A King had citizens living in a village ten miles from his palace. This village had fantastic spring water, and the King ordered the villagers bring him some every day.

The villagers, however, were greatly annoyed and inconvenienced having to make the lengthy trip. One day, a village leader said: "I'm going to go to the King and ask him to issue a decree stating that from now on, the distance from our village to the palace will only be one mile. This will make our task much easier."

After hearing the man's request, the King gladly complied and issued the decree—much to the delight of the villagers. One of them, however, remarked: "What difference will that make? The distance will remain the same—only the name will change!"

Nevertheless, the villagers still believed in the King's decree.

People who cling too much to names and words often act like those villagers.

•••

34

Man Yelling At Water

A thirsty traveler spotted a wooden conduit with water running in it, and drank until he was satiated. After finishing, he held up his hand and announced to the water: "I'm done drinking. Stop running." As the water continued to run, the man grew angry and yelled: "I'm done drinking, and I just told you to stop! Why are you still running?"

A bystander noticed this and remarked: "Why don't you just leave the water instead of yelling for it to stop flowing?"

The man's behavior is similar to people who, rather than doing what is necessary, just verbally demand that something happen, and then become angry when it doesn't.

• • •

35

Lots Of Work, Little Reward

A man spent months carving and polishing a large rock into a toy cow. He did an enormous amount of work, yet it resulted in very little.

This is analogous to people who work hard merely to excel others in fame. If they were motivated by the supreme fruits instead of fame, the payoff for their efforts would be much greater.

•••

36

Spotting Gold

A man mistakenly thought he spotted gold in a pond, and dove in to retrieve it. After coming up empty handed and stirring up the water's mud, he got out of the pond and waited for the mud to settle. When it did, he once again saw what he thought was gold, and dove in to get it but yet again met with failure.

He got out and sat by the pond for a few minutes, and then his father came walking by and said: "Why are you all wet and tired?"

The man replied: "I spotted gold in the lake, and I dove in to get it, but all to no avail."

The father looked at the pond, which had settled down again, and saw the gold, but could tell that it was actually a reflection of gold on a tree behind them. He turned around and looked at the tree, and the gold was there. He showed it to his son, and the son got the gold.

The same stands for the people who indulge in falsehood. The actual reward lies elsewhere but they are busy following their desires to gain worldly pleasures.

•••

37

The Fast Eater

The day after their marriage, a newlywed couple was eating a meal together—and for no apparent reason, the husband was wolfing down his food like there was no tomorrow.

One day, his wife said to him: “My beloved husband, no one is going to steal your food. Why don’t you slow down and enjoy it?”

The husband snappily replied: “That’s my secret. I can’t tell you.”

Upon hearing this, the wife became even more curious about her husband’s bizarre eating habits, and asked once again in an affectionate tone. Finally, the husband replied: “I eat like this because my family has eaten quickly for as long as we can trace back our history. I’m just following our custom.”

Many people act like this man. Rather than considering whether what they’re doing is right or wrong, they simply say, “This is how our group has done things for as long back as we can remember, and that is why we do it now,” and they persist in these actions without modifying them, all the way until their death.

•••

38

The Monkey And The Pea

A monkey ran down from a tree and snatched a huge handful of some people's peas. As he ran back up the tree, one of the peas fell from his hands. He tried to grab it, but in his attempt to catch that one pea, he dropped all of the others he was carrying. They all fell to the ground, and some animals ate them.

This is like a person who maintains some righteousness, but then upon making one small mistake, he doesn't deal with it properly, and foolishly throws all righteousness away.

•••

39

The Goldsmith

Imagine a goldsmith that is using tongs and a furnace to melt gold. If he constantly makes the fire too hot, the gold will get too hot. If he constantly sprays too much water on it, the gold will not be hot enough. If he constantly takes it out to examine it, it will never become refined. However, if he does all these things but each at their suitable time when needed, and he knows the nature of gold, he will have no problem at all in molding and refining it.

Just like that example, any practitioner needs to attend to these three qualities: focus, determination, and composure. If he properly attends to these things at the right time and circumstance, his mind will become pliant, brilliant, and pure, just like gold.

•••

40

The Guide

Several merchants hired a guide to lead them to a certain harbor.

On the way, the group came across a famous shrine; and the merchants, knowing that it was customary to make a human sacrifice whenever passing it, decided to sacrifice the guide.

Afterwards, they continued on their journey minus the now-dead guide; and without him, they got lost, wandered the desert for several days, and eventually died of thirst.

Correct actions are our guides to the Way, similar to how a human guide can lead travelers to a destination. Some, however, sacrifice correct actions, and end up lost.

•••

41

The Starving Man And The Camel

A King noticed that one his servants, a very poor man, had gradually become thin and weak. In order to help him, the King gave him a camel that had just died.

The man began to skin the camel, but found that his knife was not sharp enough. As he searched for a whetstone, someone informed him that there was one at the top of a nearby tower.

And so, the man went to the tower and climbed it, found the whetstone, and used it to sharpen his knife. After doing so, he went back down and continued skinning the camel, but his knife dulled again.

Again, he climbed the tower, sharpened his knife, and went back down—and again, he skinned the camel some more until his knife became dull.

And then after continuing this pattern a few more times and growing exhausted from the trips, he later decided to drag the camel all the way up the tower and skin it there.

But he obviously would have been best off by bringing the whetstone down to the camel in the first place, and saving himself all the unnecessary work.

…

42

Wealthy Man's Spit

Long ago in a small town, everyone competed to gain the favor of an extremely wealthy man. Even if he spitted, someone would hurry to honor him by putting out the spit with their foot. One villager, however, never got the opportunity to even do that. So one day, he decided that since everyone beat him to stepping on the spit before it reached the ground, he would carefully observe the wealthy man, and step on the spit just as it was leaving his mouth. Greatly pleased with his plan, he followed through with it the next day—but he ended up kicking the man right in the face and injuring him severely! Greatly angered, the other yelled: "You must be a lunatic! Why did you just kick me in the mouth?"

The reply was: "I did it to gain your favor, Sir. When you spit, everyone else rushes to step and put it in the ground, but I am always too late. So I stepped on it even before it left your mouth. And now that you know my reason, surely you are pleased by what I did."

The man's mistake was that his timing was wildly off. There is a proper time for everything, and if a person wants to force a benefit before the proper time for it has arrived, it will result in problems.

•••

43

The Arrow

Someone wounded by a poisoned arrow would not delay in removing it instead of trying to first find out the exact details of who shot it, the reason that person shot it, where the arrow was manufactured, etc. If he attended to all of that before pulling out the poisonous arrow, he would probably die.

In this same way, dealing with the life situations that we experience at hand should be prioritized over concern about understanding things.

•••

44

The Patient Elephant

While the Blessed One was residing in the Jetavana, there was a householder living in Sravasti known to all his neighbors as patient and kind, but his relatives were wicked and contrived a plot to rob him. One day they came to the householder and by worrying him with all kinds of threats took away a goodly portion of his property. He did not go to court, nor did he complain, but tolerated with great forbearance the wrongs he suffered. The neighbors wondered and began to talk about it, and rumors of the affair reached the ears of the brethren in Jetavana. While the brethren discussed the occurrence in the assembly hall, the Blessed One entered and asked: “What was the topic of your conversation?” And they told him.

Said the Blessed One: “The time will come when the wicked relatives will find their punishment. O brethren, this is not the first time that this occurrence took place; it has happened before,” and he told them a world-old tale: “Once upon a time, when Brahmadatta was king of Benares, there was a cub born to an elephant in the Himalaya region. He grew up strong and big, and ranged the hills and mountains, the peaks and caves of the torturous woods in the valleys. Once as he went he saw a pleasant tree, and took his food, standing under it. Then some impertinent monkeys came down out of the tree, and jumping on the elephant's back, insulted and tormented him greatly; they took hold of his tusks, pulled his tail and disported themselves, thereby causing him much annoyance. The gentle beast, being full of patience, kindliness and mercy, took no notice at all of their misconduct which the monkeys repeated again and again.

"One day the spirit that lived in the tree, standing upon the tree-trunk, addressed the elephant saying, 'My dear elephant, why don't you put up with the impudence of these bad monkeys?' And he asked the question in a couplet as follows:

'Why do you patiently endure each freak
These mischievous and selfish monkeys wreak?'

"The gentle beast, on hearing this, replied, 'If, Tree sprite, I cannot endure these monkeys' ill-treatment without abusing their birth, lineage and persons, how can I walk in the eightfold noble path? But these monkeys will do the same to others thinking them to be like me. If they do it to any rogue elephant, he will punish them indeed, and I shall be delivered both from their annoyance and the guilt of having done harm to others.' Saying this he repeated another stanza:

'If they will treat another one like me,
He will destroy them; and I shall be free.'

"A few days after, the gentle beast went elsewhere, and another elephant, a savage beast, came and stood in his place. The wicked monkeys thinking him to be like the old one, climbed upon his back and did as before. The rogue elephant seized the monkeys with his trunk, threw them upon the ground, gored them with his tusk and trampled them to mincemeat under his feet."

After this discourse one of the brethren rose and asked leave to propose a question and when the permission was granted, he said: "I have heard the doctrine that wrong should be met with wrong and the evil doer should be checked by being made to suffer, for if this were not done evil would increase and good would disappear. What shall we do?"

Said the Blessed One: "Nay, I will tell you. You who have left the world and have adopted this glorious faith of putting aside selfishness, you shall not do evil for evil nor return hate for hate. Neither think that you can destroy wrong by retaliating evil for evil and thus increasing wrong. Leave the wicked to their fate and their evil deeds will sooner or later in one way or another bring on their own punishment."

And the Tathagata repeated these stanzas:

"Who harms the man who does no harm,
Or strikes at him who strikes him not,
Shall soon some punishment incur
Which his own wickedness begot,-

One of the gravest ills in life,
Either a loathsome dread disease,
Or sad old age, or loss of mind,
Or wretched pain without surcease,

Or conflagration, loss of wealth;
Or of his nearest kin he shall
See someone die that's dear to him,
And then he'll be reborn in hell."

•••

45

Blind Men And The Elephant

A number of disciples went to the Buddha and said: "Sir, there are living here in Sravasti many wandering hermits and scholars who indulge in constant dispute, some saying that the world is infinite and eternal and others that it is finite and not eternal, some saying that the soul dies with the body and others that it lives on forever, and so forth. What, Sir, would you say concerning them?"

The Buddha answered: "Once upon a time there was a certain king who called to his servant and said: 'Come, good fellow, go and gather together in one place all the men of Sravasti who were born blind... and show them an elephant.' 'Very good, Sire,' replied the servant, and he did as he was told. He said to the blind men assembled there, 'Here is an elephant,' and to one man he presented the head of the elephant, to another its ears, to another a tusk, to another the trunk, the foot, back, tail, and tuft of the tail, saying to each one that that was the elephant.

"When the blind men had felt the elephant, the king went to each of them and said to each: 'Well, blind man, have you seen the elephant? Tell me, what sort of thing is an elephant?'

"Thereupon the men who were presented with the head answered: 'Sire, an elephant is like a pot.' And the men who had observed the ear replied: 'An elephant is like a winnowing basket.' Those who had been presented with a tusk said it was a ploughshare. Those who knew only the trunk said it was a plough; others said the body was a grainery; the foot, a pillar; the back, a mortar; the tail, a pestle, the tuft of the tail, a brush.

"Then they began to quarrel, shouting, 'Yes it is!' 'No, it is not!' 'An elephant is not that!' 'Yes, it's like that!' and so on, till they came to blows over the matter.

"And the king, O brethren, was highly delighted.

"Just so are these preachers and scholars holding various views blind and unseeing.... In their ignorance they are by nature quarrelsome, wrangling, and disputatious, each maintaining reality is thus and thus."

Then the Exalted One rendered this meaning by uttering this verse of uplift:

"O how they cling and wrangle, some who claim

For preacher and monk the honored name!

For, quarreling, each to his view they cling.

Such folk see only one side of a thing."

•••

46

The Burning House

"Now I will tell you a story," the Buddha said, "Once there was a man of great wealth who had many children. One day, a fire broke out at his place and was burning down his mansion. The man was absent from his place and when he returned, he found that his children were so distracted by their own thoughts and actions, that they had not realized the house was burning down and were thus still inside the house. The father screamed: 'Get out, my dear children! Come out of the house! Quickly!' But the children were so absorbed in their games that they did not heed his warning.

"Knowing that the children were fond of interesting playthings, the anxious father called out to them: 'My beloved children, I have some marvelous things here for you to play with; quickly come out of the house and get them!' This time they listened to his cries and eager to play with the new toys, they rushed out of the burning house. But instead of the promised toys, the father gave them a cart much better than any he had described – a cart draped with precious stones and pulled by white bullocks.

The important thing being that the children were saved from the dangers of the house on fire."

In this parable the father, of course, is the Buddha and sentient beings are the children trapped in the burning house. The Burning House represents the world burning with the fires of lust, greed and hatred. The teachings of the Buddha are like the father getting the boys to leave their pleasures for a greater pleasure, Nirvana.

•••

47

Ignorance Intensifies The Suffering

Once the Buddha was seated with his bhikshus in the shade of many beautiful sala trees. He picked up a small piece of earth, held it between his thumb and forefinger, and asked: "Bhikshus, if we compare this piece of earth with Gayashirsa mountain, which is larger?"

"Of course, Gayashirsa is much larger, Lord."

"It is like that, O Bhikshus. For those who have arrived at Understanding thanks to their study and practice of the Dharma, their suffering is almost nothing compared with the suffering of those who are submerged in ignorance. Ignorance magnifies suffering by millions of times.

"Bhikshus, suppose someone is struck by an arrow. He will feel pain. But if a second arrow strikes him at the very same spot, the pain will be much more than just doubled. And if a third arrow strikes him at that same spot again, the pain will be a thousand times more intense. Bhikshus, ignorance is the second and the third arrow. It intensifies the pain.

"Thanks to understanding, a practitioner can prevent the pain in himself and others from being intensified. When an unpleasant feeling, physical or mental, arises in him, the wise man does not worry, complain, weep, pound his chest, pull his hair, torture his body and mind, or faint. He calmly observes his feeling and is aware that it is only a feeling. He knows that he is not the feeling, and he is not caught by the feeling. Therefore, the pain cannot bind him. When he has a painful physical feeling, he knows that there is a painful physical feeling. He does not lose his calmness, does not worry, does not fear, and does not complain. Thus the feeling remains a painful physical feeling, and it is not able to grow and ravage his whole being."

• • •

48

Purity Of Water

Once the Blesssed One in company with the Brotherhood, was traversing the Malla country and he came to Thuna, a Brahmin village, in the Malla country. And the Brahmin householders of Thuna, on hearing that the Samana Gautama was traversing the country in the company of his monks and had arrived at Thuna, they filled up the well to the brim with grass and straw, so that these shaven monks, as they called them, should not obtain water to drink.

And the Blessed One, leaving the road, went to the foot of a tree and drawing near sat down on the prepared seat and while thus sitting he said to Ananda: "Bring me, I pray, Ananda, some water from that well."

When these words had been spoken, the venerable Ananda said to the Blessed One: "That well, Sire, has been filled up to the brim with grass and straw by the Brahmin householders of Thuna, so that we may not obtain water to drink." A second time the Blessed One said to the venerable Ananda: "Bring me, I pray thee, Ananda, some water from that well." And Ananda yet again gave the same reply. But when a third time the Buddha said thus, Ananda said: "So be it, Sire," in assent to the Blessed One, and he went to the well, taking with him a bowl.

And when he arrived at the well he found that all the grass and straw had been removed and that it was full to the brim, even to overflowing, of pure, clear, translucent water. And the thought occurred to the venerable Ananda: "How astonishing, how marvelous is the mighty power and great strength of the Perfect One, that on my arrival all the grass and straw were removed and the well was full to the brim, even to overflowing, of clear, pure, translucent water."

And taking some water in the bowl, he went to where the Blessed One was and said to the Buddha: "How astonishing, how marvelous, is the mighty power and great strength of the Perfect One, by which the grass and straw was removed... Drink, Exalted One, of the water: Drink, Happy One, of the water."

And the Blessed One, in this connection, breathed forth this solemn utterance:

"When there is water everywhere, what need of a well?

When desire has been uprooted.

In search of what should a man wander?"

•••

49

83 Problems

A man worried by his problems of the worldly life came to see the Buddha. He had heard that the Buddha was a great teacher and he thought the Buddha might be able to help him straighten those out.

He told the Buddha that he was a farmer. "I like farming," he said, "but sometimes it doesn't rain enough, and my crops fail. Last year we nearly starved. And sometimes it rains too much, so my yields aren't what I would like them to be."

The Buddha patiently listened to the man.

"I am married too," said the man. "My wife is good… I love her in fact. But sometimes she nags me too much. And sometimes I get tired of her."

The Buddha listened quietly.

"I have kids," said the man. "Good kids, too… but sometimes they don't show me enough respect. And sometimes…."

The man went on like this, laying out his difficulties and worries. Finally, he wound down and waited for the

Buddha to say the words that would put everything right for him.

Instead the Buddha said: “I can’t help you.”

“What do you mean?” said the astonished man.

“Everybody has got problems.” said the Buddha. “In fact, we have all got 83 problems. Each one of us. Eighty-three problems and there’s nothing you can do about it. If you work really hard on one of them, maybe you can fix it—but if you do, another one will pop right into its place. For example, you’re going to lose your loved ones eventually. And you’re going to die someday. Now there’s a problem, and there’s nothing you or I, or anyone else, can do about it.”

The man became furious. “I thought you were a great teacher,” he shouted. “I thought you could help me! What good are your teachings then?”

The Buddha said: “Well, maybe they will help you with the 84th problem.”

“The 84th problem?” inquired the man. “What’s the 84th problem?”

Answered the Buddha: “You want to not have any problems.”

•••

50

The Outcast

Once when the Blessed One was dwelling at Sravasti in the Jetavana, he went out one day on his alms round in the city. And he happened to approach the house of a Brahmin priest when the fire of an offering was blazing upon the altar.

But the priest said: "Stay there, O shaveling; stay there, O wretched samana; you are an outcast."

To this, the Blessed One replied:

"Who is an outcast? An outcast is the man who is angry and bears hatred; the man who is wicked and hypocritical, he who embraces error and is full of deceit.

"Whosoever is a provoker and is avaricious, has evil desires, is envious, wicked, shameless, and without fear to commit wrong, let him be known as an outcast.

"Not by birth does one become an outcast, not by birth does one become a Brahmin; by deeds one becomes an outcast, by deeds one becomes a Brahmin."

Thus saying the Blessed One moved on while the Brahmin priest looked at him with his mouth wide open, as he had been completely outwitted by the Buddha.

•••

51

Four Kinds Of Merit

There was a rich man who used to invite all the Brahmins of the neighborhood to his house, and giving them rich gifts offered sacrifices to the gods.

And when the Blessed One came to know of this, he said:

"If a man each month repeat a thousand sacrifices and give offerings without ceasing, he is not equal to him who but for one moment fixes his mind upon righteousness."

The Blessed One continued: "There are four kinds of offering: first, when the gifts are large and the merit small; secondly, when the gifts are small and the merit is also small; thirdly, when the gifts are small and the merit large; and fourthly, when the gifts are large and the merit is also large.

"The first is the case of the deluded man who takes away life for the purpose of sacrificing to the gods, accompanied by carousing and feasting. Here the gifts are great, but the merit is small indeed.

"The gifts are small and the merit is also small, when from covetousness and evil heart a man keeps to himself a part of that which he intends to offer.

"The merit is great, however, while the gift is small, when a man makes his offering from love and with a desire to grow in wisdom and in kindness.

"Lastly, the gift is large and the merit is also large, when a wealthy man, in an unselfish spirit, gives donations and establishes institutions for the best of mankind to enlighten the minds of his fellow-men and to administer unto their needs."

•••

52

Deeds And Rituals

From ancient times it is a belief held by some cultures that prayers and rituals could be used to circumvent the effects of evil deeds and even secure a place in the heaven.

Once a village headman named Asibandhakaputra, who was a lay follower of Nigrantha Nataputra, came to the Buddha and enquired about the effectiveness of these prayers and rituals.

And the Blessed One said: "Suppose, headman, a person would hurl a huge boulder into a deep pool of water. Then a great crowd of people would come together and assemble around it, and they would send up prayers and recite praise and circumambulate it making reverential salutations, saying, 'Emerge, good boulder! Rise up, good boulder! Come up to high ground, good boulder!'

"What do you think, headman? Because of the prayers of the great crowd of people, because of their praises, because they circumambulate it making reverential salutations, would that boulder emerge up, rise up, and come up to the high ground?"

"No, Venerable Sir," replied the headman.

“So, too, headman, if a person destroys life, takes what is not given, engages in sexual misconduct, speaks falsely, speaks divisively, speaks harshly, chatters idly, one who is covetous, full of ill-will, and holds wrong view, even though a great crowd of people would come together and assemble around him, and they would send up prayers and recite praises and circumambulate around him making reverential salutations, saying, ‘With the breakup of the body, after death, may this person be resurrected in a good destination, in a heavenly world’, still with the breakup of the body, after death, that person will be resurrected in a state of misery, in a bad destination, in the nether world, in hell.”

Then the Buddha explained to him that one who followed the ten courses of wholesome conduct would have made causes to be resurrected in a heavenly world, regardless of what prayers or rituals others might perform to spitefully send that person to hell. The Buddha compared this with a pot of oil that was to be broken in a deep pool, for the oil would always rise to the surface even if people were to foolishly pray for it not to, just so the one who committed good deeds would be resurrected in heaven.

•••

53

The Gift

When the Buddha observed the ways of society, he noticed that much misery came from malignity and foolish offenses. So, one day, he addressed a gathering of lay people and said:

“If a man does me wrong, I will return to him the protection of my ungrudging love; the more evil comes from him, the more good shall go from me; the fragrance of goodness always comes to me, and the harmful air of evil goes to him.”

A foolish man learning that the Buddha observed the principle of great love which commands the return of good for evil, came forward and abused him. And consequently, the lay followers of the Buddha became furious and had their fists tightly closed, but remained quiet only because of the respect they had for their Master.

And all the while the Blessed One patiently endured the abuse of the wicked man.

When he had finished his abuse, the Blessed One asked him, saying: “Tell me, if a man declined to accept a present made to him, to whom would it belong?”

"In that case the present would belong to the man who offered it," replied the fool.

And the Blessed One said: "So you have railed at me, but I decline to accept your abuse, and request you to keep it yourself. Will it not be a source of misery to you? As the echo belongs to the sound, and the shadow to the substance, so misery will take the evil-doer without fail."

The abuser made no reply, and the Blessed One continued: "A wicked man who reproaches a virtuous one is like one who looks up and spits at heaven; the spittle soils not the heaven, but comes back and defiles his own person. The slanderer is like one who flings dust at another when the wind is contrary; the dust does but return on him who threw it. The virtuous man cannot be hurt and the misery that the other would inflict comes back on himself."

Hearing it, the abuser went back ashamed, but he returned later and apologized to the Buddha, and then took the threefold refuge.

•••

54

Loving-Kindness

The Buddha, with the intention of teaching his disciples the importance of the cultivation of loving-kindness, told them a story, saying: "Once upon a time there lived in Sravasti a lady named Videshika, who was reputed gentle and meek, and mild. She had a maid servant named Darkie, a bright girl, an early riser and a good worker. 'I wonder,' thought Darkie, 'whether my mistress, who is so well spoken of, has really got a temper of her own which she does not show or whether she has got no temper at all? Or do I do my work so well, that though she has got a temper, she does not show it? I will try her.'

So next morning she got up late. 'Darkie! Darkie!' cried the mistress.' 'Yes, madam,' answered the girl. 'Why did you get up so late?' 'Oh, that's nothing, madam.' 'Nothing, indeed, you naughty girl!' thought the mistress, frowning with anger and displeasure.

'So she has got a temper, though she does not show it,' thought the maid: 'It is because I do my work so well that she does not show it; I will try her further.' So she got up later next morning. 'Darkie! Darkie!' cried the mistress.

'Yes, madam,' answered the girl. 'Why did you get up so late?' 'Oh, that's nothing, madam.' 'Nothing, indeed, you naughty girl!' exclaimed the mistress, giving vent in words to her anger and displeasure.

'Yes,' thought the maid, 'she has got a temper, though she does not show it because I do my work so well; I will try her yet further.' So next morning she got up later still. 'Darkie! Darkie!' cried the mistress. 'Yes, madam,' answered the girl. 'Why did you get up so late?' 'Oh, that's nothing, madam.' 'Nothing, indeed, you naughty girl, to get up so late!' exclaimed the mistress, and in her anger and displeasure she picked up the lynch-pin and struck the girl on the head with it, drawing blood.

With her broken head streaming with blood, Darkie roused the neighborhood with shrieks: 'See, lady, what the mild one has done. What for? Just because her only maid got up late, she was so angry and displeased that she just jumped with the lynch-pin to strike her on the head and break it.'

"As a result, the lady Videshika got the reputation of being violent, anything but meek and mild.

"In the like manner, a monk may be gentle and meek, and mild enough so long as nothing unpleasant is said against him. It is only when unpleasant things are said against him that you can test if he has loving-kindness–fellowship in him."

[And the Blessed One continued:]

“I do not call a bhikshu Charged with the spirit of loving-kindness if he shows it only to get clothes and food. Him only do I recognize as a true bhikshu whose loving-kindness springs from the Dharma.

“None of the means employed to acquire religious merit, O monks, has a sixteenth part of the value of loving-kindness. Loving-kindness, which is freedom of heart, absorbs them all; it glows, it shines, it blazes forth.

“And in the same way, O monks, as the light of the stars has not a sixteenth part of the value of the moonlight, but the moonlight absorbs it and glows and shines and blazes forth; in the same way, O monks, none of the means employed to acquire religious merit has a sixteenth part of the value of loving-kindness. Loving-kindness, which is freedom of heart, absorbs them; it glows, it shines, it blazes forth.”

•••

55

The Raft

The Buddha explained the proper attitude to take towards the Dharma, through the famous parable of the raft, by saying thus:

"Monks, I shall show you how the Dharma is similar to a raft, being for the purpose of crossing over, not for the purpose of grasping. Listen and attend closely to what I shall say."

"Very good, Venerable Sir!"

"Monks, suppose a man in the course of a journey saw a great expanse of water, whose near shore was dangerous and fearful, and whose farther shore was safe and free from fear, but there was no ferry-boat or bridge going to the far shore. And he thought: 'There is this great expanse of water…Suppose I collect grass, twigs, branches, and leaves and bind them together into a raft, and supported by the raft and making an effort with my hands and feet I get safely across to the far shore.'

"And he acted likewise and got safely across to the shore. Then, when he had arrived at the far shore, he might think thus: 'This raft has been very helpful to me…Suppose I were to host it on my head or load it on my shoulder, and then go wherever I want.'

"Now, monks, what do you think? By doing so, would that man be doing what should be done with that raft?"

"No, Venerable Sir," replied the disciples.

[And the Blessed One continued:]

"By doing what would that man be doing what should be done with that raft?

"Here, monks, when that man got across and had arrived at the far shore, he might think thus: 'This raft has been very helpful to me…Suppose I were to haul it onto dry land or set it adrift in the water, and then go wherever I want.'

"Now, monks, it is by doing so that the man would be doing what should be done with that raft.

"So I have shown you how the Dharma is similar to a raft, being for the purpose of crossing over, not for the purpose of grasping.

"Monks, when you know the Dharma to be similar to a raft, you should abandon even good states, how much more so bad states."

•••

56

Does God Exist?

One day, in the early morning, Gautama Buddha was sitting in a garden quietly with his disciples. A man arrived silently and stood in the shadows, that man was a great devotee of Lord Rama. He would always chant Rama's name and contemplate on Rama's greatness. He was old and close to his last years. Even after many years of dedicated spiritual effort he was not realized.

He wanted to know for sure if there is a god or not? When he heard about the realized one (Buddha), he came to get his doubt cleared. When he felt nobody would notice him talking to the Buddha, he asked: "O Enlightened One, please tell me the truth! And truth only. Is there a god?"

Buddha, from his intuition, knew that man to be a great devotee of Lord Rama; he looked at the man with seriousness and said: "No, my friend. There is no god."

Buddha's disciples that were gathered there were very relieved and joyous to finally know the truth that there was no god. They all started muttering between them, sharing what the Buddha had just told. Whenever a disciple had asked that question to Buddha before, he would become silent. So the disciples were in great confusion.

It was getting late in the evening, and once again the disciples came back and sat around the Buddha.

There was a materialist who had been an atheist all his life, he had convinced thousands of people that there was no god, he used to go to the priests and scholars and defeat them in the argument about god.

He too was getting old and little suspicion arose in him, "what if there is god? Isn't it waste of my life to spread the 'NO GOD' message if there in actuality is god?" He was eaten by this doubt, so finally decided to know the truth and sought the enlightened one.

He slowly came up to where Buddha was sitting, and asked: "They say you are enlightened, Please tell me if there is GOD?"

Buddha, knowing that man to be an atheist, said with a firm voice as if he was of firm conviction: "Yes, there is God." Hearing it, Buddha's disciples once again were back to confusion.

For the polytheists and for those who believe in the incarnations, there is no True God. But for those who deny the Oneness and Supremacy of GOD, there is in actuality a True God.

•••

OTHER NOTABLE WORKS BY THE AUTHOR:

(1) WISDOM OF THE BUDDHA (A COLLECTION OF HIS TEACHINGS)

(2) BUDDHA AS PROPHET (A TRUE BIOGRAPHY)

(3) THE SUFI KING OF HINDOSTAN

(4) THE WAY OF THE SUFIS (A JOURNEY INTO THE LIVES OF THREE SAINTS OF ISLAM)

(5) TRUTH ABOUT AVATARS

(6) STORIES OF THE PIOUS (THE SUFI MORALS)

(7) WISDOM OF PERSIA (A TREASURE-TROVE OF MORAL STORIES)

• • •

Printed in Great Britain
by Amazon

26497750R00078